# my first bicycle book

# my first bicycle book

### A fun guide to bicycles and cycling activities
### for children aged 7 years +

**Susan Akass**

CICO **kidz**

For George, for his practical advice.

Published in 2013 by CICO Kidz
An imprint of Ryland Peters & Small
519 Broadway, 5th Floor, New York NY 10012
20–21 Jockey's Fields, London WC1R 4BW
www.rylandpeters.com

10 9 8 7 6 5 4 3 2 1

A CIP catalog record for this book is available from
the Library of Congress and the British Library.

ISBN: 978-1-78249-037-1

Printed in China

Editor: Clare Sayer
Designer: Barbara Zuñiga
Photographer: Gavin Kingcome
(pages 4, 7, 58, 61, 62, 69, and 71)
Stylist: Sophie Martell
Animal artworks: Hannah George
Step artworks: Rachel Boulton

RPS
CICO
BOOKS
For digital editions, visit
www.cicobooks.com/apps.php

# Contents

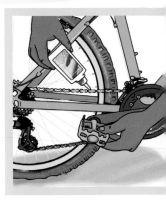

# Introduction

Cycling is great! On a bike you can zoom; on a bike you can try tricks; on a bike you can go on expeditions or have competitions with your friends. Cycling keeps you fit and healthy, teaches you to make good decisions, and gives you skills and independence.

**My First Bicycle Book** is to make sure that your bike gets used, instead of being shut up in the garage or shed, gathering dust and cobwebs. It's all about giving you ideas for fun things to do on your bike (but not on the road). What this book can't do is to teach you to ride a bike (you can only learn that on an actual bike!) or how to ride safely on roads, which you need to learn from an experienced adult or from a proper road safety training course (see page 111 for more information).

The book is divided into four chapters. The first, Biking Basics, tells you all the important things you need to know to start cycling—what kind of bike to choose, how to wear your helmet properly, where to cycle, and lots more. Chapter Two, Bike Maintenance, starts you on the journey to being able to maintain your own bike with some fun and easy maintenance tasks. Chapter Three is full of exciting activities to do on your bike, from making handlebar streamers to creating an obstacle course. Chapter Four gives you some simple and enjoyable science experiments to try out, which will help you to understand how your bike works.

# Project levels

**Level 1**
These are simple projects or activities that even a beginner cyclist can do.

**Level 2**
These projects and activities may be a little more challenging.

**Level 3**
You need to be quite confident on your bike to tackle these or you may need help from an adult.

Everyone should try and read all of Chapter One, because it contains some really important information to help you keep safe while having fun on your bike. In the last two sections of Chapter One and the other chapters, we have graded the activities or projects with one, two, or three smiley faces. Level one activities or projects are for those of you who have only just learnt to ride a bike. Level two is for those of you who are getting more confident and want to try out new challenges. Level three activities and projects are for those who, when they get on their bikes, feel they are up for anything and everything!

So— ready, steady, go! Get out your bike and get cycling!

## Chapter 1
# Biking basics

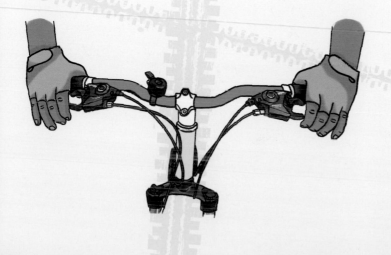

# What kind of bike should I have?

So you have learned to ride a bike! Your stabilizers have been taken off and hung up in the garage. You can get going, zoom around, and stop without falling off—and you really love cycling. Now your first bike is getting to be too small and a bit babyish. What bike should you go for next?

There are two main types of kids' bikes—mountain bikes and BMX bikes. Before you decide what to get, you need to think about where and how you will be using your bike.

- Mountain bikes are for kids who want to go somewhere on their bikes—whether it's on sidewalks (pavements), bike trails, or on rough ground over fields and through woods.

- Kids' mountain bikes come with a range of different specifications: some have no gears, some have five gears, others have eighteen gears; some have no suspension, some front suspension only, and some dual suspension; some are made of steel, some of lighter metals. The more complicated the bike is and the lighter it is, the more money it will cost.

- If you are just going to use your bike for having fun around your neighborhood, the simpler bikes will be fine; but if you are going for longer rides on your bike, good gears are essential and suspension makes for a much more comfortable ride.

- Mountain bikes come in boys' and girls' styles— the girls' frames are sometimes more V-shaped so that you can step through them. The other differences are really only the colors and the names, which are more girly for girls' bikes!

- The size of bike you get depends on how tall you are. Don't be tempted to get one that is too big for you so that you can grow into it. You won't feel safe and stable if it's too big.

## CHILDREN'S BIKE SIZING CHART

| Rider height or age | | | Size suggested |
|---|---|---|---|
| Feet and inches | Centimeters | Age (years) | Wheel diameter |
| 4 ft–4 ft 5 in. | 120–135 | 7–9 | 20 in. (50 cm) |
| 4 ft 5 in.–4 ft 9 in. | 135–145 | 9–11 | 24 in. (60 cm) |
| 4 ft 9 in. + | 145 + | 11+ | 26 in. (65 cm) |

Learn **COOL TRICKS** on a **BMX** bike!

- BMX bikes are for kids who want to begin to learn the tricks and techniques of an extreme sport, rather than using their bike to go on trips and adventures. They are not good for riding longer distances.

- BMX bikes are tough and never have gears. They are great for flinging around and having fun with your friends in your neighborhood. They are easy to keep in good working order, as there aren't many different parts.

- The handlebars on a BMX are curved and higher up from the ground than mountain bike handlebars, which are low and straight.

- The biggest wheel size on a BMX bike is 20 in. (50 cm), even for adults, so a BMX bike can last you longer than a mountain bike, which you will probably grow out of after a few years.

# Mountain bikes

Mountain bikes are designed to be ridden over rough ground, so they have tough, wide, knobbly tires and may have front and rear suspension for a comfy ride. You may want to ride long distances on a mountain bike, so they usually have gears to make riding up hills easier. They have flat handlebars.

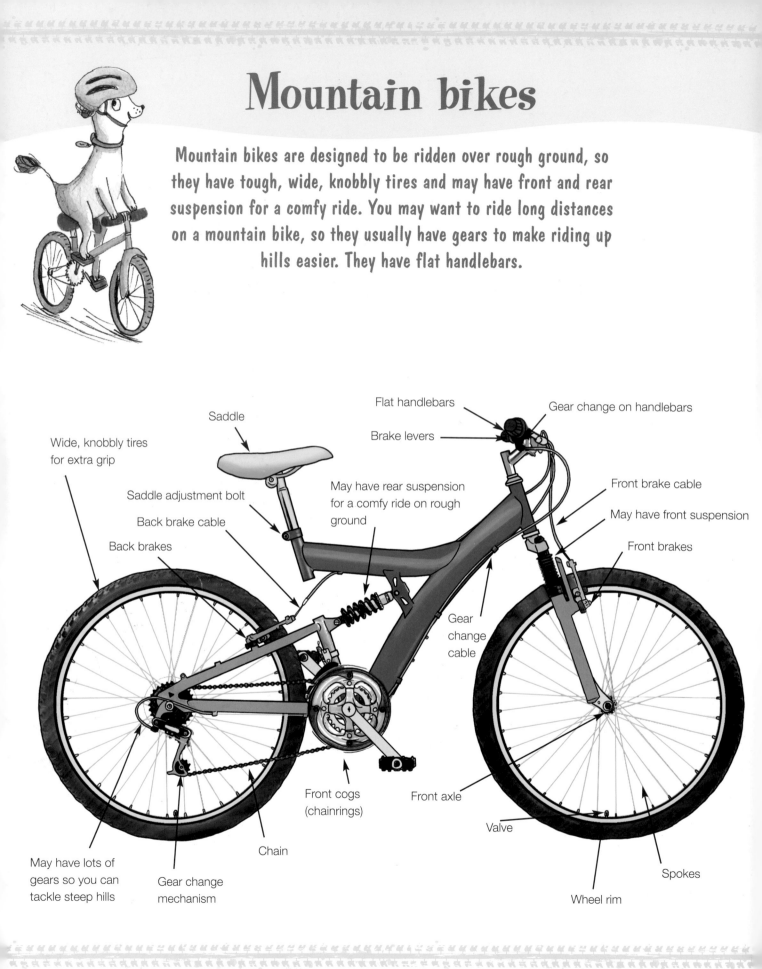

Saddle

Wide, knobbly tires for extra grip

Saddle adjustment bolt

Back brake cable

Back brakes

Flat handlebars

Brake levers

May have rear suspension for a comfy ride on rough ground

Gear change on handlebars

Front brake cable

May have front suspension

Front brakes

Gear change cable

May have lots of gears so you can tackle steep hills

Gear change mechanism

Chain

Front cogs (chainrings)

Front axle

Valve

Wheel rim

Spokes

# BMX bikes

BMX bikes are sturdy and simple. They are designed for racing over challenging circuits, with lots of bumps and jumps, or for doing tricks. They are not designed for going on long bike rides, so they don't have gears or suspension. They have low saddles and high handlebars. They are ideal bikes to have if you want to have fun around your neighborhood and to learn tricks and skills. Because they don't have many parts, they are easy to maintain.

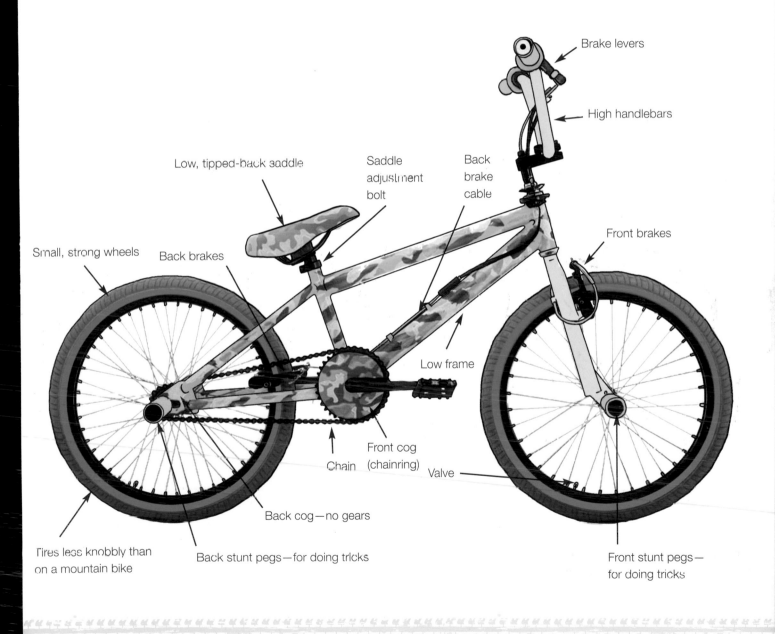

Brake levers

High handlebars

Low, tipped-back saddle

Saddle adjustment bolt

Back brake cable

Front brakes

Small, strong wheels

Back brakes

Low frame

Chain

Front cog (chainring)

Valve

Back cog—no gears

Tires less knobbly than on a mountain bike

Back stunt pegs—for doing tricks

Front stunt pegs—for doing tricks

# Adjusting the saddle height

Before you ride anywhere, you need to make sure that your saddle is the correct height. If it's too high, you won't be safe; it it's too low, you will find that pedaling is much harder work. You will probably need an adult to help you adjust your saddle, especially if the nut and bolt is stiff and difficult to undo. (Remember that on a BMX bike your saddle should be lower than on a mountain bike.)

**You will need**

A correctly sized hex or Allen key (you should have got one with your bike)

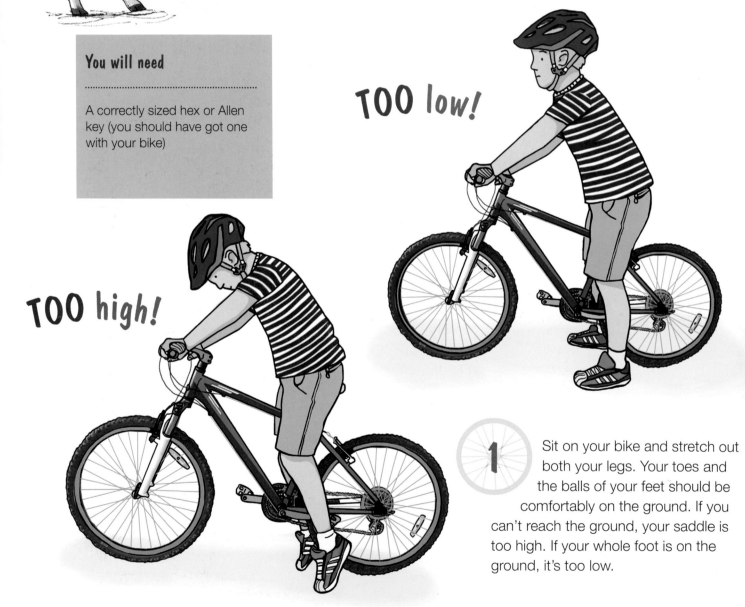

**TOO low!**

**TOO high!**

1 Sit on your bike and stretch out both your legs. Your toes and the balls of your feet should be comfortably on the ground. If you can't reach the ground, your saddle is too high. If your whole foot is on the ground, it's too low.

**2** Now put one foot on the pedal when it is at its lowest position. Your leg should be slightly bent. If it is very bent, your saddle is too low.

## JUST right!

**3** To adjust the saddle height, look underneath the saddle. The saddle is attached to a tube that fits into the frame of your bike. On the top of the frame, there will be a nut and bolt. You will need a hex or Allen key to undo the nut. (Some more expensive bikes may have a lever, which you simply need to pull out.) When the bolt is loose, wiggle the saddle up or down to the correct position. When you raise the saddle height, be careful not to pull it out beyond the safe limit. This is shown by a mark on the saddle stem, which you should **not** be able to see.

**4** Check that the saddle is pointing exactly forward in line with the frame, and then tighten the nut again.

**5** Sit on the saddle again to make certain that you have got the height just right.

Get your SADDLE height right!

# Always wear a helmet

Some people think helmets aren't cool, but those are the people who don't understand that a helmet can save your life. Even bumping your head when a stationary bike tips over can be very dangerous, so you should wear a helmet every time you ride your bike. Make sure you get a helmet that fits you well and that you really like. The cooler it is, the more you will want to wear it! Here's how to make sure that you are wearing it properly.

## You will need

A cool bike helmet (see Choosing a helmet, page 21)

Someone to help you adjust the straps

**1** Put on the helmet. It should sit flat on your head, with the front just above your eyebrows. It should never be tilted back.

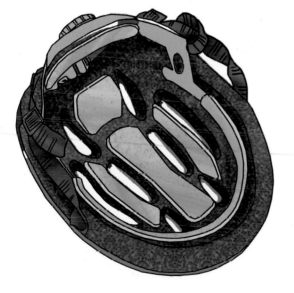

**2** The helmet will come with a choice of thick or thin foam panels to go inside. If it feels loose on your head, fit the thicker foam panels on the inside. Some helmets also have a "dial" at the back, which you can turn to tighten or loosen them.

**3** Ask an adult to adjust the sliders on both straps to form a "V" shape under and slightly in front of your ears. Lock the slider if possible.

**4** Next ask the adult to help you to adjust the chin strap so that the buckle is just under your chin, with one or two finger's width of space between the buckle and your chin. Always buckle up your helmet.

### Tip

Take care of your helmet—just dropping it onto a hard surface can weaken it, so it won't protect you as well in an accident. If you do have a fall and bang your helmet, always buy a new one—you may not be able to see them, but tiny cracks in the helmet will mean you're not protected next time.

**5** Now check the fit:

• Open your mouth wide in a big yawn! The helmet should pull down tight on your head. If it doesn't, go back to step 4 and tighten the chin strap.

• Try rocking your helmet backward. If it rocks more than two fingers above your eyebrows, unbuckle it and shorten the front strap by moving the slider forward. Buckle, retighten the chin strap, and test again.

• Try rocking it forward. If it rocks into your eyes, unbuckle it and tighten the back strap by moving the slider back toward the ear. Buckle, retighten the chin strap, and test again.

**6** When you have got it just right, roll the rubber band, if there is one, down to the buckle to hold the straps in place and to stop the buckle from slipping. All four straps must go through the rubber band and be close to the buckle.

## Choosing a helmet

There are some really fun helmets around these days, many of them in bright go-faster colors or with your favorite characters on them. There are two main types. Traditional bike helmets have a hard, streamlined outer shell and an inner shell made from polystyrene. They usually have lots of air vents to keep you cool while you're cycling along. Skate-style helmets are popular with BMX bikers—they have a rounder shape, a hard outer plastic shell, and fewer vents.

# What should I wear?

You don't need to wear stretchy lycra like the riders in the Tour de France when you ride a bike. Of course, you always need to wear a helmet, but there are a few other things you can wear that will make cycling safer and more comfortable.

**1** Shorts and T-shirts are the best clothes for general biking. Shorts won't catch on the chain, which jeans or pants (trousers) can do.

**2** Wearing trainers, not sandals, means your feet are protected. Trainers with hook-and-loop (Velcro) fastenings are better than ones with laces, as loose laces can get caught in chains.

**3** Fingerless, padded gloves are comfy on the handlebars and will protect your hands if you fall.

**4** Adventurous BMX and mountain bike riders are more likely to come off their bikes, so wearing long-sleeved tops and pants (trousers) as well as knee and elbow pads will protect you from cuts and grazes. Make sure that trousers are not loose, otherwise they may get caught in the chain.

**5** If you are going on longer rides with your family, padded cycle shorts can stop you getting a sore backside!

**6** If adults ever take you out cycling on roads, you should wear a high-visibility jacket so that drivers can see you.

# Where can I ride my bike?

Once you have learnt to ride your bike, that's where the real fun begins. At first you are going to be wobbly and nervous, so you will need to practice, practice, practice until your bike becomes part of you.

There are many different places where it is safe and fun to ride your bike, but there are two really important rules to remember.

**1** Never, ever, cycle on the road unless you are with an adult or have your parents' permission.

**2** Always watch out for other people who are walking, cycling, or enjoying other activities on the same tracks as you.

Many of the best places for cycling will be some way from your home. You will need an adult to drive you there and you will probably need to take your bike on a bike rack. Find details about fun places to ride your bike online or talk to people at your local bike shop who may have maps and leaflets. These are some ideas for where you can ride your bike:

## • Around your home
This is the best place to start, because you can do this on your own and practice a bit every day. Some of you may be lucky enough to live in places well away from main roads where there are wide sidewalks (pavements), off-road tracks, fields, or waste ground where you are allowed to play with other children from your neighborhood. You may even have an open space with ditches and hillocks on which you can plan bike courses and challenges. Wherever your local cycle spot is, remember: never cycle on roads to get there, however quiet they are, and always stop and get off your bike when you need to cross a road.

## • Parks
Many parks will allow children to cycle on the paths that run through them. You may be able to ride your bike there on your own or, if an adult takes you, you can leave them enjoying some peace and quiet on a park bench while you ride circuits of the park. Set up some cones for practicing skills or try some wheelies

on the grass (see page 78). Always be careful of other users in parks, especially elderly people, children who are much younger than you, or dogs. If a dog runs after you, do not try to out-pedal it. The dog will be faster than you are and may cause you to crash. Instead, stop, put the bike between you and the dog, and shout, "Go away!" The owner will hopefully be somewhere near and will fetch the dog.

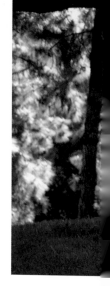

### • Railway paths
Where railways have been shut down, some old railway tracks have been turned into paths, which people use for walking, for wheelchairs, and for cycling. Since trains can't go up steep hills, railway tracks were always built with very gentle slopes, which make them great for cycling on. These tracks are good for day trips—get a group of adults and children together, plan an expedition to somewhere interesting near the path, and take a picnic.

### • Canal paths
Canal paths are even flatter than railway paths. They were built for horses to walk along as they towed long boats along the canals. Nowadays the boats have engines, so everyone can enjoy using the paths for walking or cycling. There is always plenty to see beside a canal—wildlife, boats, fishermen, the people who live on canal boats—so these are great for a slower day out. Don't forget your picnic!

### • Cycle routes
There may be cycle routes in your area, which include cycle lanes on or beside roads. These are safer than riding on roads, but you should still ask an adult's permission before you ride on them, as you will be riding close to traffic and you could wobble into it. You will also need to know how to use road junctions properly. Sometimes the cycle lanes disappear altogether, leaving you riding on a main road—which can be quite scary!

### • Off-road trails
Sometimes you will find dirt roads, unpaved tracks, and forest paths in your area, but be careful—these are sometimes rough, steep, and hard work to cycle on. Find out which are suitable for family bike rides.

### • Vacations (holidays)
If your family are jetting off on vacation, obviously you can't take your bike—but if you're driving, some places may be ideal for cycling. Camping trips are great for this. Many campsites have very strict, very slow speed limits for cars, which means it is safe to ride on the roads and on the recreation areas around the site. Plus you are almost guaranteed to find other kids with bikes to have fun with. If your whole family is into cycling, there are often campsites in areas where there are cycle trails and you can all go off together for longer trips. Ask your family about activity vacations set in large parks, where you stay in chalets that are

connected to all the various activities by bike trails. If your family is renting a vacation home away from busy roads, check out whether there are good places to ride your bike.

## • Family fun rides

More and more of these are taking place — sometimes just for fun and to get people on their bikes, but more often than not to raise money for charity. Part of a town center may be closed to traffic so that families can get onto the roads in safety. There is often a great atmosphere and sense of fun when lots of people join in the same activity. Look out for posters in your local bike shop or advertisements in your local newspaper or events site.

## • BMX parks and clubs

If you have become a confident BMX rider and need more of a challenge, find out if there is a BMX park near you. Some parks need you to have your parents' permission before you can use them. If you do go to one, be sure to wait your turn and avoid getting in the way of more experienced riders. You could also join a BMX club—these have members as young as three years old, so even beginners can join them. They will help you develop your skills and tricks and will organize races and competitions.

# Braking

Braking safely is the first thing you should learn when you ride a bike. It's no good being able to zoom down a hill if you can't stop at the bottom! These are a few tips for safe braking.

- Always check your brakes before you set out for a bike ride (see page 48).

- When you brake, always use both brakes together. In the US and Europe, the front brake is usually on the left; in the UK, it is usually on the right. If you use the front brake without the rear brake, the bike can tip you forward over the handlebars.

- When you brake, squeeze both brake levers evenly—don't snatch at them too hard or too fast, or you could skid or go over the handlebars.

- If you need to brake hard, keep your weight back and low.

- Be very careful on steep hills. The faster you go, the longer it will take to stop and the more difficult it becomes to avoid unexpected hazards such as holes or rocks. Keep to a safe speed by braking then releasing every few seconds.

CAN you stop SAFELY?

# What's up ahead?

Anticipation—looking to see what is up ahead—is the key to safe biking. Remember that if you are cycling fast, and you have to make sudden stops or swerves, you could easily skid and crash. So be sure that you see what is coming. These are the main things you need to look out for:

- Roads up ahead—if you are coming along a trail or sidewalk (pavement), be sure you know when there are roads up ahead. You don't want to zoom onto a road in front of moving traffic.

- Potholes and stones—hitting these at best shakes you up or, at worst, tips you over.

- Sudden bends—be sure that you are not going down a hill so fast that you can't turn at the bottom.

- Wet surfaces—your tires won't grip as well on these and your brakes won't work properly either.

- Gravel, ice, and wet drain covers—the wheels can't grip on these and you can skid and crash, especially on bends.

- Mud and deep sand—these can stop your bike dead!

- Other people—they can step into your path unexpectedly, so have a bell to warn them you are coming.

- Other cyclists—stay a reasonable distance behind friends in case they stop suddenly and cause a pile-up. To make sure there is a safe stopping distance between you and another friend on a bike say, "one elephant, two elephants," before you start off behind someone else. Also watch out for other cyclists coming toward you and give them plenty of room.

- Dogs—if a dog runs after you, do not try to out-pedal it. The dog will be faster than you are and may cause you to crash. Instead, stop, put the bike between you and the dog, and shout: "Go home!"

- Overhanging branches—you don't want a faceful of leaves and twigs or, even worse, to hit a branch.

# The attack position

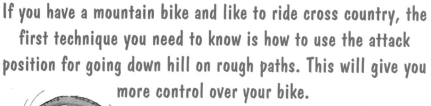

If you have a mountain bike and like to ride cross country, the first technique you need to know is how to use the attack position for going down hill on rough paths. This will give you more control over your bike.

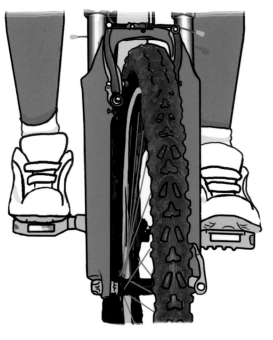

**1** Bring your pedals round so that your feet are level.

**2** Stand up on your pedals. Keep your weight on the pedals— don't lean too hard on the handlebars.

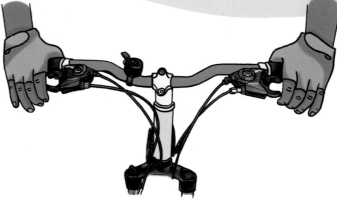

**3** Cover your brakes with your fingers so that you are always ready to brake and you can keep control of your speed.

**4** Keep your knees and elbows bent but relaxed— this means they act as shock absorbers, so the bumps don't go through to your body.

## ATTACK that hill!

**5** When going down steep hills, move the weight of your body backward by moving your bottom back behind the saddle.

# Using gears

When you first learn to ride a bike, all you can think about is balancing and heading in the right direction. As your skills grow, you will soon learn that, on a mountain bike, gears are your best friends. Gears allow you to ride at high speed on flat paths, but also to make it up steep hills without getting too puffed out. Using gears correctly needs practice, but these tips should help.

**1** Look at your bike to find out how many gears you have. More is not necessarily better! You may have one, two, or three large cogs (called chainrings or front sprockets) attached to your pedals and you will have about five or six smaller cogs attached to your back wheel. The chain runs between the front and back cogs and there are complicated mechanisms to move the chain between the cogs. An 18-speed bike has three chainrings at the front and six cogs at the back (3 x 6 =18).

**2** Now look at your handlebars: this is where you will find the gear shifters.

These come in lots of different designs, from levers to twist shifts. The one on the right handlebar controls which of the back cogs the chain is on. This is the one you will use most. The one on the left handlebar controls which of the front chainrings the chain is on  (If you only have one chainring, you'll only have one shifter on the right handlebar.) The gear shifters have numbers on them. High numbers are for when you are traveling fast on flat paths or down hills; low numbers are for going up hills. (To understand more about how gears work, see page 100.)

**3** Remember: you cannot change gear unless you are moving and pedaling. If you only have one chainring, you only need to think about a right shifter—but even if you have three chainrings, for most of the time you should be using the middle one (number 2) and you should hardly have to think about your left shifter.

When you are pedaling, you shouldn't have to push too hard on your pedals. If you come to a hill and pedaling is getting to be hard work, use your right gear shifter to change to a lower number gear. To do this, ease off, so you are not pushing hard on the pedals, then click the shifter by one click while you keep pedaling. If the hill gets steeper, move down another gear.

**4** When you come to flatter ground or start going downhill, you will suddenly find your legs going round too fast – this is the time to change up a gear. Keep pedaling and click the shifter the other way, to a higher number, by one click. As you gain more speed, change up another gear. Move smoothly from one gear to the next as you gain speed. Your legs should always feel comfortable as you pedal—not working too hard and not turning too fast!

**5** To use gears well, you need to think ahead. Remember to change down a gear (keep pedaling!) before you find it difficult to pedal up a hill. If you are pressing too hard on the pedals, it is very difficult to change gear. Also, when you have been pedaling fast on a high gear and are coming up to a stop, remember to change down to a lower gear (keep pedaling!) before you stop. If you don't, it will be very hard to get going again.

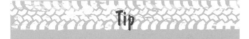

**Tip**

Never try to change gear while you are standing up on your pedals.

 **6** If you have more than one chainring, you can change down to the smallest one (number 1) for really hilly rides, or to the biggest one (number 3) for long, flat stretches when you really want to get up speed.

**7** There are some combinations of gears that just don't work because the chain is stretched between them on too much of a diagonal. So, if you are on gear 1 on your left gear shifter, you shouldn't be on gear 6 on your right, or if you are on gear 3 on the left shifter, you shouldn't be on gear 1 on the right. That's why it is easiest to stay on the middle chainring.

# Bike maintenance

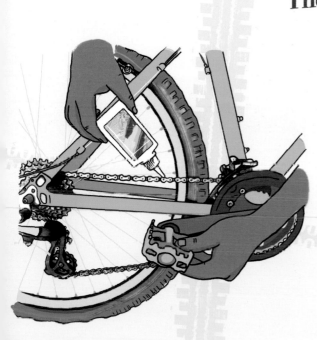

# Pumping up tires

Bike tires that are too soft make bike riding hard work and they are also more likely to puncture. Bike tires go soft gradually, even when you are not using your bike, so it is really important to check that they are hard enough and to pump them up, if they need it, before you begin riding.

**You will need**

A bicycle pump

**1** To test whether your tire is hard enough, try pushing it in with your thumbs. You shouldn't be able to push it in at all, but as your thumbs are probably not very strong, you should ask an adult to try, too.

**2** If the tire feels soft, get your bicycle pump. There are many different types—here we've shown a foot pump and a hand pump.

**3** Find the valve of your tire. This is the small tube that pushes through the metal inside your bike wheel. Unscrew the cap from the top of the valve and put it somewhere safe, like your pocket. (A cap is very easy to lose and you don't want to lose it because it protects the valve.) The valve lets air go in but doesn't let air come out. You can let air out by pushing the small pin on the inside of the valve with your nail or the end of a pen— you will hear a loud hiss as the air rushes out.

**4** Attach the head of the pump to the valve. Different pumps have different attachments—some just push on firmly, some have a tube that screws into the end of the pump and then screws onto the valve. Tall stand pumps have a lever to lock them onto the valve. You will hear a small hiss of air escape as you attach the pump head to the valve.

**5** Pump up the tire—this will test your muscles but it's fun! Keep checking to see if the tire is hard enough.

## Are your TIRES hard?

**6** When the tire is really hard, take off the pump (a little air may escape as you do this, but don't worry). Replace the valve cap and get started on the other tire.

**7** When you are pumping up your tires, check that they are not worn out. If the pattern of tread on the rubber is worn smooth or the sides of the tires are cracked, you will need new tires.

# Mend that puncture

All bikes get punctures at some time. Mending a puncture is quite difficult—you need to know how to remove a bike wheel and you need to have strong fingers to remove the tire from a wheel and then to replace it. However, you can help an adult to find the puncture and repair it once the tire is off.

**1** Ask an adult to remove the wheel from the bike. Check all around the tire to see if there is anything sticking into it such as a nail or a piece of glass, which might have caused the puncture. If there is, pull it out carefully—you may need a pair of pliers!

**2** Find the valve poking through the rim of the wheel. Take off the valve cap and put it somewhere safe, such as your pocket. Let any remaining air out of the tire by pushing in the pin in the middle of the valve with something thin, such as a nail or a matchstick. You will hear the air rush out.

**3** Ask the adult to pull the tire off the rim using some tire levers. Feel inside the tire and you will find the soft, squidgy inner tube, which is the part of tire that holds the air. The valve is attached to the inner tube. Push the valve up through the hole in the wheel rim and then carefully pull the inner tube out of the tire.

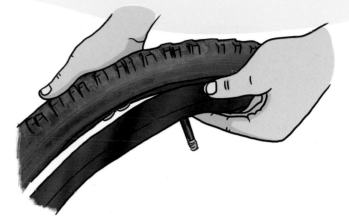

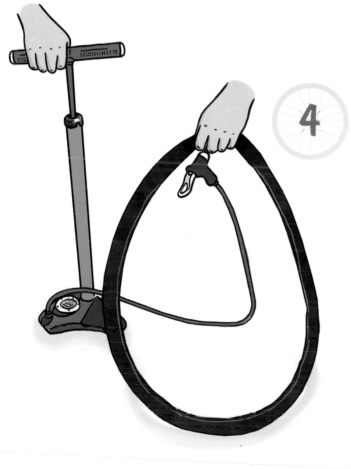

**4** Attach the bicycle pump to the valve and pump up the inner tube until it is round and inflated—it doesn't need to be hard.

# Find the HOLE!

**5** Listen for the sound of air escaping. You may find the puncture straight away. If you don't, use the bowl of water. Push the tube under water and watch for a trail of bubbles escaping from the tube.

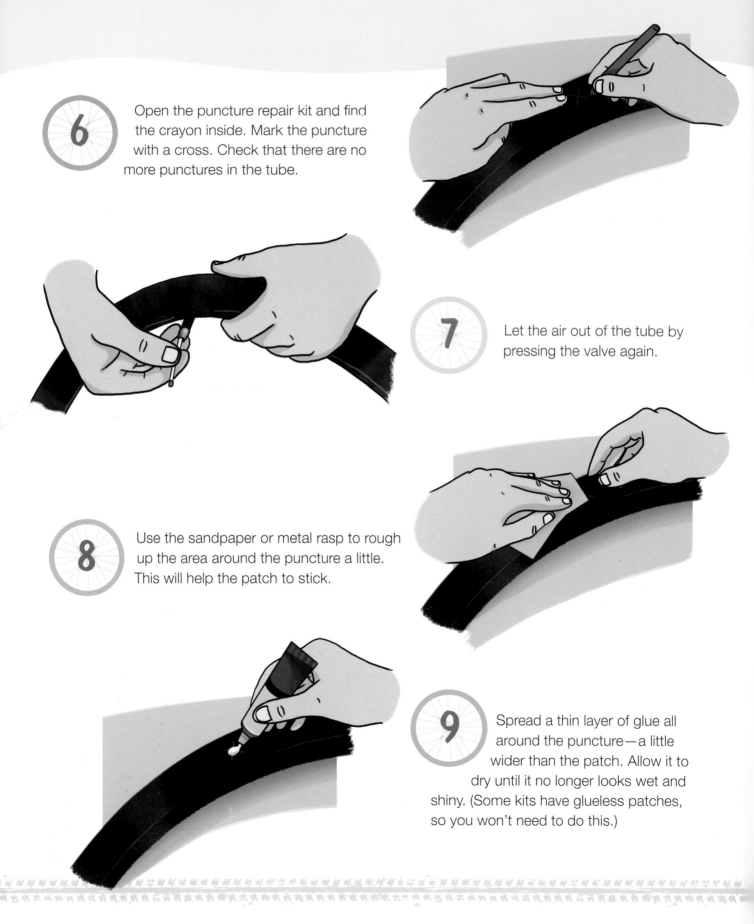

**6** Open the puncture repair kit and find the crayon inside. Mark the puncture with a cross. Check that there are no more punctures in the tube.

**7** Let the air out of the tube by pressing the valve again.

**8** Use the sandpaper or metal rasp to rough up the area around the puncture a little. This will help the patch to stick.

**9** Spread a thin layer of glue all around the puncture—a little wider than the patch. Allow it to dry until it no longer looks wet and shiny. (Some kits have glueless patches, so you won't need to do this.)

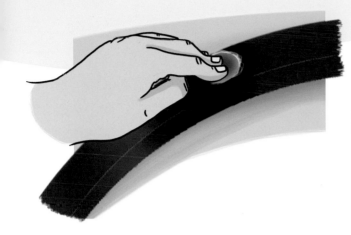

**10** Peel the plastic backing from the patch. Be careful not to touch the sticky adhesive surface underneath, which makes a seal with the glue on the tube. Press the sticky side down onto the puncture. Press firmly down onto a hard surface to make sure it seals all the way round.

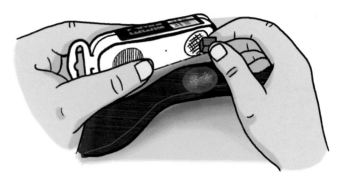

**11** Take the chalk and sandpaper or grater and grate some chalk all over the patch and the area around it. This will stop any extra glue sticking to the inside of the tire.

**12** Before you put the tire back, have a good look around the inside of the tire to check if there is anything sticking through that could cause another puncture. Sometimes thorns, nails, and pieces of glass don't show on the outside. Don't run your fingers around the inside, as you could cut yourself.

**13** Ask the adult to replace the inner tube in the tire and the tire back on the bike. Then pump up the tire (see page 38) and replace the valve cap.

# Lubricate for an easier ride

To keep your bike running smoothly it will need to be lubricated. Lubricants make moving parts slip easily over one another (see page 96) and a well-lubricated bike is much easier to ride. Some lubrication will need to be done by experts, but it is a simple job to lubricate your chain so that it runs smoothly over the cogs. If your chain starts to squeak, that is the time to lubricate. Don't do it too often, as the lubricant can clog up the chain.

**You will need**

A light bike lubricant with dripper top (available from bike shops)

A dry rag (tear up an old tee shirt)

 **1** Carefully clean and dry the chain (see page 51).

 **2** On the top of the chain, between the front and rear cogs, drip one tiny drop of lubricant into each tiny link of the chain.

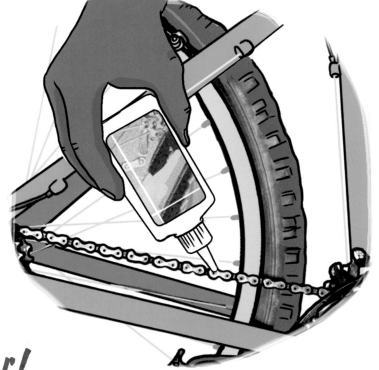

## SMOOTH operator!

**3** Turn the pedals backward a little. This will move the chain on so that the next part is on top. Lubricate that. Keep going until you have lubricated the whole chain.

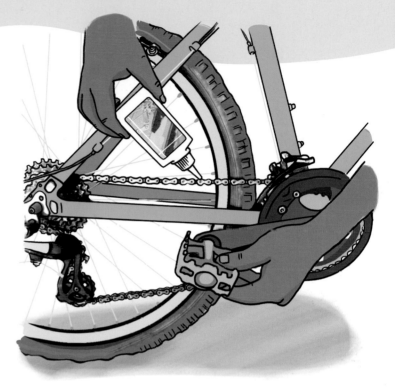

 **4** Now turn the pedals backward lots of times, so that the chain turns and the lubricant works its way into all the links.

**5** Finally use the cloth to wipe the chain, wiping off any excess lubricant on the outside of the chain. As before, turn the pedals after wiping each section to make sure that you have wiped it all. This is important because dirt will stick to any lubricant that runs out of the links and it will clog up the chain.

# Put your chain back on

You are riding happily along and suddenly your pedals no longer seem to work—you turn them but they don't push the bike along. Whoops—your chain has come off! This is very annoying, but on a mountain bike it is easy to put it back. (On a BMX bike it may be more difficult and you will have to ask someone to help you.)

**1** Stop pedaling the moment you notice your chain has come off, so that it doesn't get jammed.

## Whoops—
## my CHAIN came off!

**2** Lean your bike against a wall or tree. Try to find a rag or a tissue to hold the chain with—that way, you can keep your fingers clean.

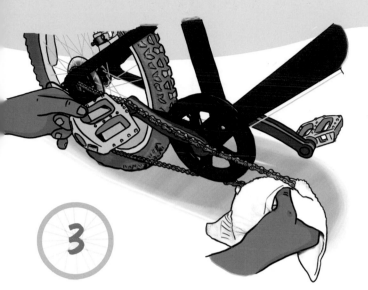

**3** Now pick up the chain near the bottom of the front cog. Hook a few of the links onto a few of the teeth on the cog.

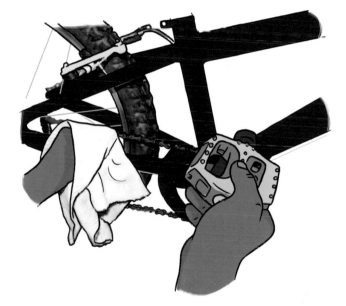

**4** While you hold the chain up against the cog wheel with one hand, very slowly turn the pedal backward with the other. As it turns, the front cog should pick up the links of the chain until it is all back in place. You can start riding again.

**5** If your chain keeps coming off, you will have to have it adjusted by an adult who knows how to do it or you will need to take your bike to a bike repair shop.

# Check your brakes

If you can't slow down or stop, it means you are not safe on a bike—so checking your brakes is one of the most important things you should do. Also, if your brakes are not adjusted properly they may rub and that makes cycling hard work. These checks are easiest to do with a friend: before you go anywhere on your bikes, help check each other's brakes. If you find that your brakes are not working properly, you will need to ask an adult to help you to adjust them or take your bike to a bike shop for a service.

**1** Lift the front wheel off the ground and get a friend to give it a spin. It should keep spinning for a long time—does it? Listen! Can you hear any rubbing? If the wheel stops quickly and you hear it rubbing, it means that the brake blocks are touching the wheel rim. This will slow you down as you ride and will wear out the brake blocks. Now check the back wheel in the same way. You will need to turn the pedal to get it going. If your brakes are rubbing, you will need to have them adjusted.

 **2** If the wheels spin freely, test the brakes. Spin the front wheel in the same way as before and then squeeze the left brake lever (right in the UK). The wheel should stop dead. You should only need to pull in the lever in by about a half an inch (one centimetre) before the wheel stops. If the wheel doesn't stop OR you have to pull the lever a long way before it stops, your brakes need adjusting. Now check the back wheel with the other brake lever.

**3** Next get on your bike, cycle a little way to gain some speed, and then brake smoothly. Could you stop easily? If not, those brakes will need adjusting.

# Make sure that you can STOP!

# Keep your bike clean

Dirt and water are the enemies of bikes. Dirt can act like sandpaper and can wear away at your chain. Water causes rust, which stiffens up the moving parts of your bike such as the brake cables. So, to keep your bike working really well, you need to keep it clean and dry.

## You will need

A bucket of very warm water—not too hot or you will scald your hands

Dishwashing liquid

Two or three old rags (old tee shirts are good)

An old scrubbing brush

An old toothbrush

**1** After you have used your bike, put it away somewhere dry like a shed or garage. That way it won't end up all rusty.

**2** If your bike gets really dirty on a ride, you could hose it off before you put it away—don't use a pressure hose as this could damage some parts. Check carefully under the mudguards (if you have them). Mud can get trapped here and you need to squirt it out.

**3** When you have more time, you can give your bike a more careful clean. Fill a bucket with very warm water and add a good squirt of dishwashing liquid. Ask an adult for an old scrubbing brush, an old toothbrush, and some rags—old T-shirts are good for this. Don't use paper towels as they will end up in shreds. Tear the T-shirts into smaller pieces before you use them, so that you can wring them out easily.

**4** Wash the bike all over using plenty of water. Clean the inside rims of the wheels by using the toothbrush to poke between the spokes or by covering your finger with a rag.

**5** Last of all, but most importantly, clean the chain. Put the bike into the lowest gear, so that the chain is on the largest gear wheel at the back. Use the scrubbing brush to scrub the chain all over. When you have given it a really good scrub to get off all the dirt and grit, turn the pedals backward to move the chain round a little so that you can do the parts you couldn't get to at first. Do this several times.

**6** You should also clean the gear-changing mechanism at the back of the chain, but be gentle with this—do it carefully with a toothbrush.

**7** When everything looks clean and shiny, wipe the chain with a dry rag—you'll be surprised how much dirt will still come off it. Wiggle the links as you wipe them so that you get to bits you couldn't see before.

**8** If your chain has been squeaking, now is the time to lubricate it (see page 44).

# Be proud of your clean, shiny BIKE!

# The M-check

To stay safe and in good working order, bikes should have regular all-over maintenance checks. An adult can help you go through these checks and may be able to fix any problems. If they can't, you will need to take your bike to a bicycle repair shop.

**Saddle and saddle stem**
- saddle does not move
- saddle stem does not move
- limit mark not visible on saddle stem

**Handlebars**
- handlebars and stem are not loose

**Front brake**
- the front wheel locks when brake lever is pulled
- brake pads are not rubbing tire or wheel rim
- brake pads are not missing

**Frame**
- frame not bent or damaged

**Front tire**
- inflated
- not worn or cracked

**Rear brake**
- as for front brake

**Rear wheel**
- as for front wheel

**Rear gear**
- as for front gear

**Rear tire**
- as for front tire

**Crank and front gear**
- gear moves chain from one sprocket to another
- sprocket not bent
- crank shaft not loose
- pedals not loose

**Front wheel**
- wheel nuts or skewer are not loose
- hub bearings are not loose
- spokes are not loose

# Chapter 3
# Have fun on your bike

# Customize your bike

If you have a brand new bike you probably won't want to change it much, but if you have one that has been passed down from an older brother or sister or bought second hand, you may want to make it all your own. Here are some fun ideas to customize your bike.

**1** Glow in the dark! Change the boring, black hand grips, pedals, and stunt pegs on your BMX for ones made in fluorescent colors.

**2** Stay clean, be cool! Add mudguards to your mountain bike. Customize these and any other parts of your bike with cool stickers.

**3** Sparkle as you ride! Clip spoke-sparklers to the spokes of your bike (you can buy boy ones and girl ones). They catch the light so you stand out in the dark and make fun, tinkly sounds as you ride.

**4** Catch the wind! Add handlebar streamers to your bike—they'll stream out behind you as you zoom. (You can buy these or make your own—see page 60.)

**5** Be heard! You can buy bells and hooters in every possible design and theme—which superhero do you want on yours?

**6** Be informed! Want to know how fast and how far you have ridden? You need a bike computer.

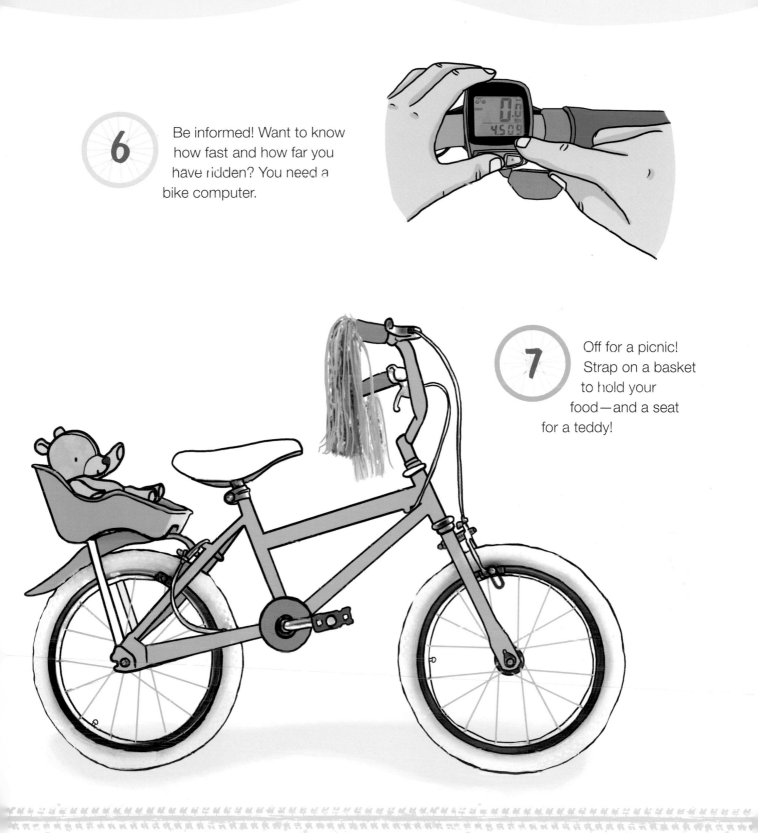

**7** Off for a picnic! Strap on a basket to hold your food—and a seat for a teddy!

# Handlebar streamers

When these streamers stream out beside you as you zoom along, they will look great and make you feel as if you are going twice as fast. Make your own with brightly colored plastic carrier bags—it's a really good way to reuse them.

## You will need

Scissors

2 long, narrow screws

2 rubber bands or some thin wire

Plastic carrier bags in different colors—bright ones are best

**1** Look at the handlebars of your bike. The rubber or plastic hand grips which cover the ends should have small holes in them. Check that your screws will push into the hole—don't push them right in yet—you might find them hard to pull out again!

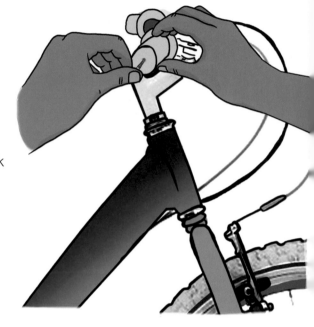

**2** Cut the top off the carrier bags so they are each about 10 in. (25 cm) from the bottom to the top.

**Tip**

You can make these any length, but be sure that they are not long enough to get tangled in your wheel.

**3**

Starting at the bottom, cut the bag into strips about ¾ in. (2 cm) wide. Each one will be doubled over, with a crease where the bottom of the bag was. Cut 20 strips.

**4** Open up the strips and lay them on top of one another in two piles of ten strips, with the creases lined up.

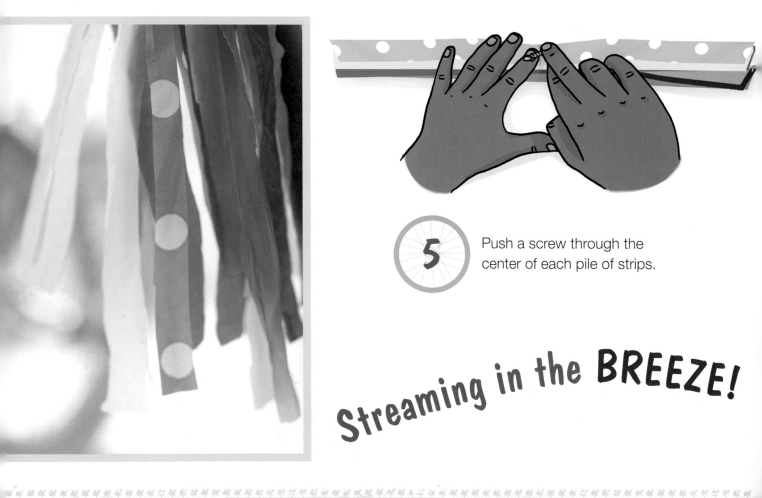

**5** Push a screw through the center of each pile of strips.

*Streaming in the BREEZE!*

**6** Push the screws into the holes in the handgrips of your bike.

**7** Pull the strips back around the screw and hold them together with an elastic band (in the same way as you would put an elastic around a ponytail in your hair).

**8** Cycle off and watch them stream back beside you as you zoom.

# Noisy flappers

Have you got a useless pack of playing cards from which you've lost some of the cards? Most families have! Here's a great use for them. Make them into noisy flappers on the back wheel of your bike.

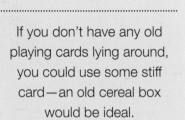

## You will need

Some old playing cards
Sticky tape

### Tip

If you don't have any old playing cards lying around, you could use some stiff card—an old cereal box would be ideal.

**1** Position one card on the back frame of your bike so that the card sticks out between the spokes. The spokes should just catch the card as the wheel turns. Stick it in place with some sticky tape on one end—the card and tape should be on top of the frame so that as the wheel turns forward the card is pushed towards the frame.

## How LOUD can you get?

**2** Ride the bike around. The faster you go the louder you will sound.

**3** When one card wears out, replace it with another.

**4** Experiment with more cards to get an even louder sound—you can have them on the front wheel as well.

# Stop right there!

Stopping exactly where you want to on a bike is not as easy as it sounds. This is a great game for developing your braking skills. You could just practice on your own but it's more fun if you make it into a competition with some friends. You need some complicated markings for this one, so it is best done on a hard surface such as a driveway— ask your parents' permission first! Never play this game on a road.

## You will need

Some chalk

A ruler

**1** Draw one long, straight line with some chalk, about 20 paces long.

**2** About 24 in. (60 cm) from the end of the line, draw another bold line across it (like crossing a T). This is the stopping line and shows you exactly where you have to stop.

**3** Draw 6 smaller lines across the main one, marking them every 4 in. (10 cm) beyond the stopping line. Then turn round and mark 6 lines every 4 in. (10 cm) before the stopping line.

**4** Your aim is to stop with the bottom of the front wheel exactly on the bold cross.

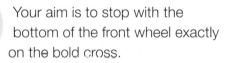
### Tip

Remember your controlled braking (see page 28). You don't want to tip over your handlebars!

**5** You start with ten points and one point is taken off for each 4-in. (10-cm) marking that the rider stops in front of or behind the stopping cross. So if you are three marks beyond the stopping cross, you lose 3 points.

**6** Start at the beginning of the line—get up some speed then try and stop exactly on the cross. Take turns with your friends—the person with the highest score wins.

## STOP right there!

# Butting bottle and ducking gate

These are some fun obstacles which you could include as part of the obstacle course ideas on pages 82–85. A butting bottle hangs so you can only just reach it with your head when you are up on your pedals. You butt it with your helmet as you cycle by. A ducking gate works the opposite way—you have the bottles dangling low so that you have to crouch right down on your bike so as not to hit them.

## You will need

7 plastic bottles with lids

Acrylic paints and paintbrushes (optional)

A nail for piercing the lids

String

Scissors

A cane about 40 in. (1 m) long

Suitable trees—see steps 3 and 7

**1** If you want your plastic bottles to look funky, remove the labels and then paint them.

**2** Make holes in the lids of all the bottles. Place the tops on a cutting board and screw into them with a nail. You will easily be able to pierce a milk bottle top this way, but other tops may be harder and you may have to ask an adult with a small drill to help if you use these.

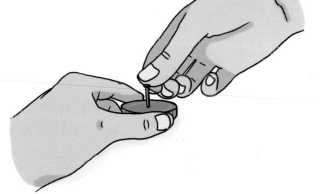

**3** For the butting bottle, find a tree with an overhanging branch that you can cycle under. The branch should be well above your head when you are standing up on your pedals. Estimate how high your branch is. The higher it is, the longer the length of string will need to be. Cut a piece of string at least twice as long as it will need to be to hang the plastic bottle at the correct height for you to butt it.

**4** Thread the string through the hole in one of the plastic bottle tops and tie a double or triple knot to stop it from pulling through. Screw the plastic bottle onto the top.

**5** You may need to get a tall adult to help you now—but don't let your adult take over the next part, as it is a fun bit! Hold tight to the end of the string, throw the bottle over the branch, and catch it.

 **6** Now ask the adult to tie the other end of the string around the neck of the plastic bottle, so that the bottle dangles at just the right height for you to butt it when you are up on your pedals. Put on your helmet and get head butting.

## Tip

To help you learn to control your bike with one hand (which is essential when you start riding on roads and need to signal which way you are turning), lower your butting bottle to shoulder height and practice hitting it with your hands—your right hand going one way, your left hand coming back.

## BUTT that bottle!

 **7** For the ducking gate, you need two trees fairly close together that you can cycle between.

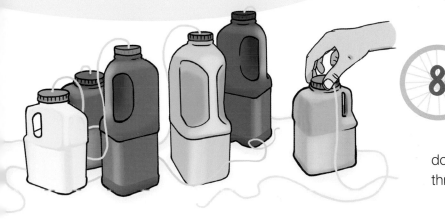

**8** Take the other six bottle plastic bottle tops and cut a length of string for each one, about 28 in. (70 cm) long. Thread a length of string through each plastic bottle top. Knot the string with double or triple knots to stop it from pulling through. Screw the bottles onto the tops.

**9** Tie the ends of the string to the cane, spacing them evenly along it.

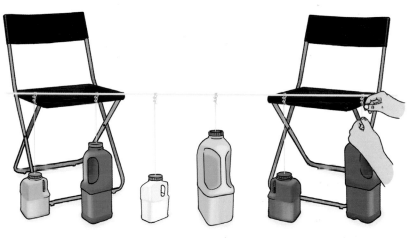

**10** Take the cane out to your trees. Securely tie a long piece of string to each end of the cane and then tie the cane so that it hangs between the trees (again, you might need a tall adult to help you do this). Make sure that the cane is high enough so that there is no chance of your head hitting it even when you are up on your pedals but low enough so that you have to duck right down to get under the bottles.

# Slow bike races

The slower you go on a bike, the harder it is to balance (see page 92 to find out why)—so a slow bike race is a lot harder than a fast one and you don't need as much space to race it! You could do a slow race on grass or on a tarmac surface such as a playground or a wide sidewalk (pavement).

## You will need

Chalk or skipping ropes

Three or more people is best—two to ride and one to be judge

A clipboard, paper, and pencil (optional)

**1** Mark out the starting and finishing lines of your course. About 30 paces apart would be about right, but it doesn't really matter. Use chalk if you are riding on a hard surface such as a driveway and skipping ropes for grass. Or use your imagination—a line of colorful leaves would do the job!

How SLOW can you go?

**2** The object of the race is to be the last to cross the finishing line. Two riders start side by side at the starting line. The judge shouts, "Ready, steady, go" and they start riding.

**3** The judge watches to see if they put their feet down and marks it on the paper if they do.

**4** The last to cross the finishing line gets ten points minus one point for each time they put their feet down. The other riders gets six points minus any points for putting their feet down.

**5** All kids take turns to act as judge and all race against each adding to their scores as they go—the person with the highest score wins.

# Tightrope tollbooth

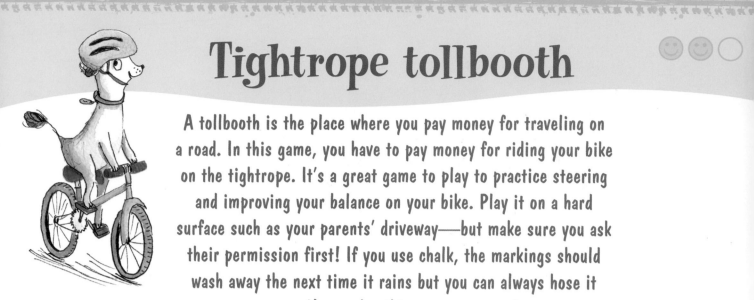

A tollbooth is the place where you pay money for traveling on a road. In this game, you have to pay money for riding your bike on the tightrope. It's a great game to play to practice steering and improving your balance on your bike. Play it on a hard surface such as your parents' driveway—but make sure you ask their permission first! If you use chalk, the markings should wash away the next time it rains but you can always hose it away. Never play this game on a road.

## You will need

Chalk

A bucket or cardboard box

A few small stones or coins—enough for you and your friends to have one each

**1** Draw one long line on the sidewalk (pavement) about 30 paces long—it can be longer or shorter depending how much room you have but it needs to be quite long to be challenging and fun. Keep it as straight as you can.

**2** Now draw another line beside it, about a handspan away. This is your cycle lane, so try to keep it the same width all the way along.

# Keep **INSIDE** the lines!

**3** Put your bucket or box at the end of the lane, just to one side of it.

**4** Take it in turns to cycle along the cycle lane and drop your stone or coin into the bucket at the end.

**5** Start with ten points. Take away one point each time someone goes outside the lines. Chalk up the scores on the sidewalk!

# Wheelies

If you have a BMX bike, you are probably really into tricks and have worked out how to do wheelies already. However, you can still do wheelies on a mountain bike and there's no reason why you shouldn't be able to do other tricks on these bikes, too. The wheelie is one of the basics, but you must be careful. Pull up too hard and you could tip right back off the bike. Always practice on soft ground.

### You will need

A correctly sized hex or allen key

**1** If you have a mountain bike, ask an adult to help you lower your seat—it should be lower than the handlebars and ideally as low as possible while letting you still ride comfortably.

**2** Find some soft grass to practice on.

**3** If you are on a mountain bike, start off in your lowest gear (you don't have to be in your lowest gear, but it helps).

**4** If you are on a mountain bike, sit on the saddle, slow down until you almost come to a complete stop, and keep your feet on the pedals. On a BMX, you may be up off the saddle.

**5** Pull back on the handlebars and start pedaling as fast as you can.

**6** Shift your weight backward and over the rear wheels, leaning back and keeping your arms straight. At first your wheel will probably just hop off the ground for a second or two. Keep practicing. As your front wheel comes off the ground, try to find the center of balance and keep it there. Don't pull back too hard.

**7** When you're done, just lean forward until you come safely back down.

## Practice OVER and over AGAIN!

# Paper boy or girl

Have you ever fancied being one of those paper delivery boys or girls who you see in movies, or even in your street, riding their bikes and flinging papers into people's front yards? Well this fun game gives you a chance to practice those skills—you'll need a few friends to play it with.

## You will need

5 or more targets—these could be laundry baskets, storage boxes, or any other large containers

The same number of old newspapers

Sticky tape

An open-topped shoulder bag

**1** Roll up the newspapers and wrap some sticky tape around each of them to keep them rolled.

 **2** Put them all in the shoulder bag.

# Aim and THROW!

**3** Set up a course with the targets along the route.

**4** The first rider sets off with the bag over his or her shoulder. At each target, he or she removes a newspaper and tries to throw it into the container.

**5** Make sure someone keeps score—you get one point for each newspaper on target.

# Obstacle course

If you are lucky enough to have a field or piece of waste ground to cycle in, you could make it much more fun by creating your own obstacle course. You must ask permission before you do any digging—your parents won't be pleased if they find a dirt ramp in the middle of their perfect lawn!

## You will need

Plastic bottles with lids

Acrylic paints in bright colors

Wide paintbrushes

Plastic carrier bags in different colors

Scissors

Garden canes or long sticks

Sticky tape

Rubber cane toppers or tiny plastic bottles (for example, mini yogurt or probiotic milk containers)

Garden spades, shovels, and a wheelbarrow (ask permission before using)

Watering can

**1** Make lots of marker cones. Remove the labels from the plastic bottles and paint them in bright colors and funky designs. Let them dry.

**2** When they are dry, pour in some water until they are about one-third full to make them bottom heavy—that way, they won't tip over so easily.

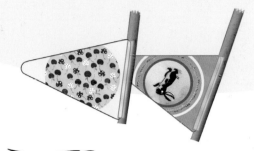

**3** Make lots of marker flags. Cut bright plastic triangles from the carrier bags and attach them to the tops of the canes with sticky tape. Push a rubber cane topper or tiny bottle onto the top of each cane to stop injuries.

**4** Go out and survey your field—are there any natural obstacles that you can use? A slope to start on is great for getting up speed. Are there any natural lumps and bumps for bumping over, or bushes and trees to steer around? Start to plan out a course with whatever you've already got there.

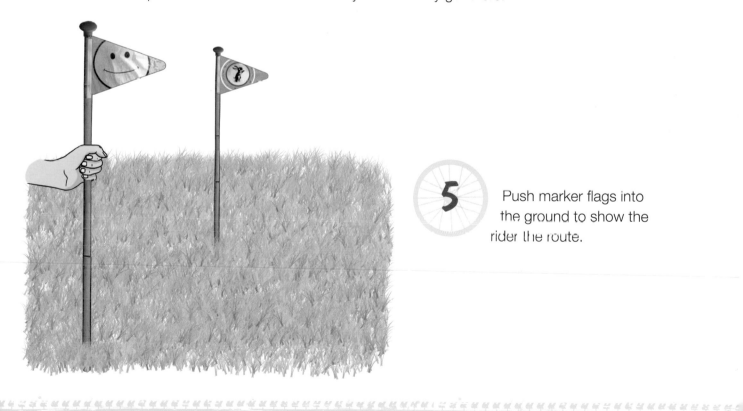

**5** Push marker flags into the ground to show the rider the route.

**6** Add a slalom to your course. Position the plastic bottles about 40 in. (1 m) apart. The rider has to zigzag between them.

# Go, go, GO!

**7** If you have permission, build a dirt ramp to jump from. This will be hard work, so you'll need some friends to help, but remember—if you are working together be careful with sharp, heavy spades. Start by choosing the position of your jump. You need a good space in front of it to get up speed and a good space behind it for landing. It will need to be about 40 in. (1 m) wide.

**8** Now get your dirt (soil). Find a good place to dig it from (remember to ask permission) and start shoveling it into the wheelbarrow. Pick out any big stones as you go. You will need lots and lots of wheelbarrows full of dirt—even for a small ramp.

**9** Pile it up where you want the ramp to be and then begin to shape it into a ramp. You don't want it too steep for your first ramp—you can always add to it and change it as your skills grow. Once you have got the shape about right, bash it down to make it solid. Then dampen it with a watering can and leave it to dry. This will make it even harder.

**10** If you still want to go on digging and have got plenty of space and enough dirt, construct a rhythm section for your course—that's a series of small mounds about 40 in. (1 m) apart for bumping over. Make these in the same way as you made the slope, dampening them and leaving them to dry at the end.

**11** Once you've made your course, you can time yourself going around it. Try to improve your time each time you go around, taking off penalty points for a foot down or an obstacle missed. Compete with friends for the "Course Champion" award!

# Bike challenge

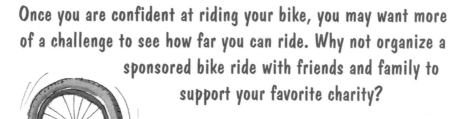

Once you are confident at riding your bike, you may want more of a challenge to see how far you can ride. Why not organize a sponsored bike ride with friends and family to support your favorite charity?

## You will need

Adults who are willing to help

A group of kids who want a bike-riding challenge

A suitable place for your course

Access to a computer

Good organizing ability

**1** Work with some adults to decide on a suitable route. Think about these things:
- It must never go onto a road. If the route has to cross a road, you will need an adult there to help you cross it safely.
- The best courses are a circuit so that you don't have to turn round to come back.
- For less experienced riders, a fairly short course that you can go round lots of times is best. Decide how far you want to cycle—it should be a challenge, but not one you can't manage.
- Courses are more fun if there are some different obstacles and places of interest along the way—for example, hills, bridges, bends, a bit of cross country.

**2** Decide which charity you want to support. Decide on a date and time for the ride. Decide how you want your sponsors to sponsor you—per lap of the circuit is easiest. Make eye-catching sponsorship forms that include all the details.

**3** Give out the forms and find out how many kids want to come on the ride. Keep numbers fairly small—if you have too many people, you may need to have permission from people who own the trails or paths, such as park authorities.

**4** Find out how many of the riders' parents would be willing to help organize the ride. Tell them that you are going to set a time limit for the course—say two hours. The adults may not want to sit around all day! For the day of the ride, ask the adult helpers to bring these things:

• Folding chairs to sit on
• Refreshments for the cyclists—bottles of water, disposable cups, and small snacks such as bananas or cookies
• A small first-aid kit
• A few tools in case of emergencies

**5** On the day of the ride, ask the adults to position themselves at turning points on the circuit, so that they can direct the riders where to go next, or by roads, if any need crossing, so that they can help the riders cross safely.

**6** The adult at the starting position should help the children check their bikes before they start. They should check their brakes and the fit of their helmets.

**7** At the start, riders should set off one at a time with about a twenty-second gap between them so that they don't all bunch up and crash. Ring your bell if you want to overtake another rider. Remember: this is not a race— go too fast and you will tire yourself out and you won't be able to ride so far.

**8** The adult who is at the starting point should mark down each time you finish a lap. This is a great opportunity to use a bike computer, If you have one, to find out exactly how far you have ridden.

## Rise to the CHALLENGE!

**9** After everyone has finished, ask them to remember to collect their sponsorship money. Once you have all the money, the easiest way to send it is to give it to your parents and ask them to make out a check (cheque) to the charity. Write a short note to go with it to say who you are and how you raised the money. Then congratulate yourself on a job well done.

### Tip

Give your friends about two weeks to collect their sponsorship money, as it will take them time to get it from all their sponsors. You might have to keep reminding them about it!

**10** Older and more experienced riders may want to ride a longer course that they only ride round once. If you do this, you will need to stay as a group with an adult cyclist riding at the front and back. That means that all the kids need to be about as fit and as good at cycling as each other. However, you should not ride too close together—you don't yet have the skills of the Tour de France riders and sudden wobbles or stops could cause pile-ups. You will also need to take along a backpack with your own drinks bottle and snacks. The adults should bring first-aid kits and tools and cell phones in case of emergencies.

# Chapter 4
# The science of bikes

# Spinning wheels

Have you ever wondered why it is so much easier to balance on a bike when you are going quickly, rather than when you are going slowly? Also why, when you stop, is it almost impossible to balance for more than a couple of seconds? This easy experiment will help you to understand.

## You will need

................................................

A bicycle

An adult to help you

**1** Ask an adult to help you take the front wheel off a bike—it's easiest to take one off a bike that has quick release levers on the wheels.

**2** Hold the wheel between your outstretched arms, with one hand gripping each of the center hubs.

**3** Try tipping the wheel to one side, then the other—it's easy, isn't it? Why wouldn't it be?

**4** Now ask someone else to spin the wheel—get it going quite fast.

**5** Now try tipping it to one side and the other, as before. What do you feel? Not so easy, is it?! The force that stops you being able to tip it is called a gyroscopic effect. Now do you understand why it's easier to balance on a moving bike?

## All in a SPIN!

# Friction

Imagine trying to cycle on an ice rink—your bike wheels would just spin round and round on one spot and never grip enough to push you forward. The way that your tires grip the path is what makes you able to ride forward. This grip is because of friction. Friction is the force that stops surfaces sliding over each other. When we say something is slippery, we mean there is not much friction on it. When we ride a bike, we want lots of friction between the tires and the road. In this easy experiment, you can see which objects have most friction on a smooth surface and begin to understand why tires are made of rubber.

## You will need

Five small objects (see Step 1)

An eraser

A smooth plank – a melamine-covered shelf is good for this.

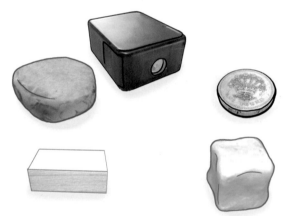

**1** Find about five small objects that are about the same size and weight as the eraser (to make it a fair test). They should all be made of different materials—for example, a metal coin, a plastic pencil sharpener, a small wooden brick from a construction set, a piece of modeling clay made into a cuboid.

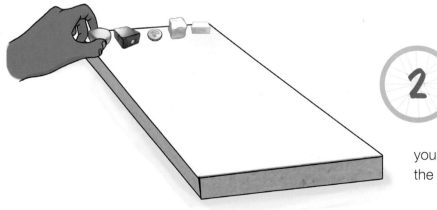

**2** Line up all the objects and the eraser on one end of the plank. You are going to slowly lift this end of the plank until the objects begin to slide. Which one do you think will slide first? Which one will grip onto the plank for the longest before it slides?

**3** Slowly begin to lift the plank at one end to make a slope. Some objects will begin to slide when there is not much slope—this means that there's not much friction between them and the slope.

**4** Keep lifting until the last object slides. There is most friction between the plank and this object. Did you get the order right when you guessed?

## Get a GRIP!

**5** Look at your bike—the tires are made of rubber, like the eraser, so they grip the road. The brake blocks are made of hard rubber, so they grip the rim of the wheels and stop them moving. Can you find other places on the bike where rubber or another grippy material is used to increase the friction on your bike?

# Let's keep moving

On some parts of your bike you need lots of grip or friction (see page 94), but on other parts you want one surface to slide smoothly over the other without sticking. If they don't slide smoothly, it will make it much harder to ride your bike — it will be like trying to pedal while you have the brakes on! There are two different ways to stop friction on a bike—lubrication and bearings. You can learn about these in two simple experiments.

## You will need

A dry bar of soap

A sink

A glass jar lid

About ten small marbles—all the same size

**1** Pick up the bar of soap. Hold it in one hand and, just by squeezing it, try to push it into the other hand. It's almost impossible.

**2** Now wet the soap. Do the same again— squeeze it from one hand to the other. It's really easy this time—in fact, the soap is quite likely to jump out of your hands and escape! This is because the water and soap have mixed to become a really good lubricant. A lubricant makes things very slippery. You should use bike lubricant (not soap!) on your chain (see page 44) to make it go round easily.

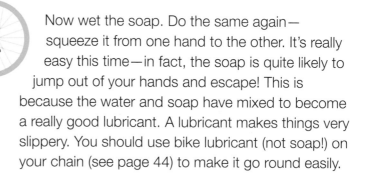

Wash the soap off your hands, dry them, and get the glass jar lid. Try giving it a push across a tabletop. Does it slide far?

Now carefully group all the marbles together under the glass jar lid. The jar lid shouldn't be too deep—the lid should sit on top of the marbles so that its edges don't touch the table.

Push the lid across the table again. How far does it go this time? It should roll along, with the marbles acting as bearings underneath.

**6** Now turn your bike over so that it is upside down. Get your front wheel spinning (but keep your fingers well away from the spokes). Count or time how long it keeps spinning for. It should go on for a really long time.

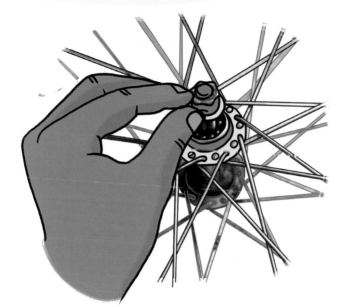

**Tip**

Ball bearings in bikes need greasing from time to time. Ask an adult to do this for you about every six months to keep your bike in tip-top condition.

# SLIP-SLIDING along

**7** Your wheel keeps spinning because there is a ring of tiny ball bearings around the axle in the middle. You could see them if you took your wheel apart. These are just like the marbles under the jar lid.

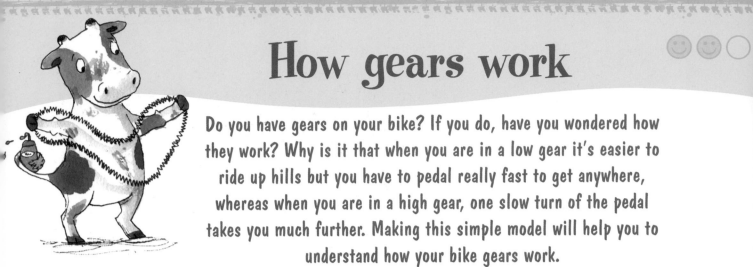

# How gears work

Do you have gears on your bike? If you do, have you wondered how they work? Why is it that when you are in a low gear it's easier to ride up hills but you have to pedal really fast to get anywhere, whereas when you are in a high gear, one slow turn of the pedal takes you much further. Making this simple model will help you to understand how your bike gears work.

## You will need

Some plastic bottle and can tops in assorted sizes—soft plastic ones are best

Some thick, long, rubber bands

Thumbtacks (drawing or mapping pins)

A piece of soft board—a cork bulletin board (notice board) is ideal, but a strong cardboard box will also work

A marker pen

Some sticky tape

 Get two bottle tops that are the same size—for example, two plastic milk carton tops. Pin one to the board, with the flat side against the board. Try to get the pin exactly through the center. Slip the rubber band over the bottle top and pull it gently until it is just a little stretched. Pin the second bottle top to the board at this point. Slip the rubber band over the second top.

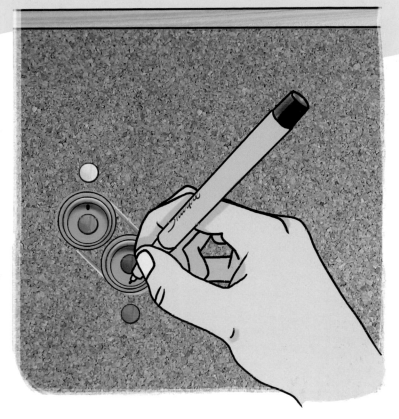

 **2** Make a mark on the board by the first bottle top and a mark on the bottle top to line up with it. Do the same for the second bottle top.

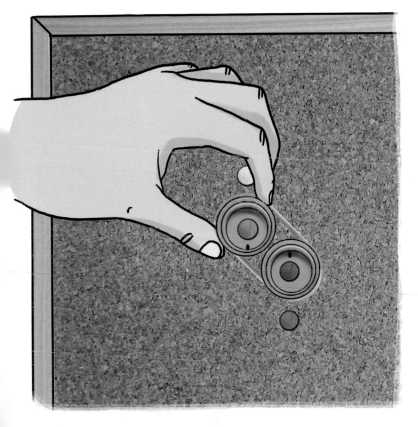

**3** Turn the first bottle top. Because of the rubber band, the second top will turn too. For every full turn the first top makes, the second top will also turn once.

**4** Now do the same with two more bottle tops. This time, use your biggest bottle top and your smallest bottle top. When you turn the big top once, how many times does the small bottle top turn? This is like being in a high gear on your bike. Your pedals are attached to cogs. With the chain around a big cog, you turn your pedal once. At the back of your bike the chain is around a small cog attached to your back wheel, so your wheel will go round lots of times and you will zoom!

**5** This time, keeping the same two tops, turn the small one. How many times do you have to turn the small bottle top before the big one completes one turn? This is more like being in a low gear on your bike. Your pedals go round lots of times, but you don't go very far.

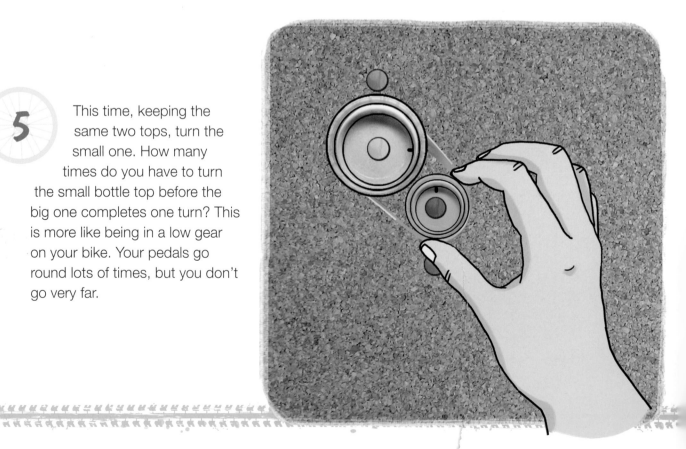

**6** Now look at your bike. Ride it and put it into a high gear. Lean it up against a wall and put the outer pedal at the top. Put a piece of sticky tape around a spoke at the top of the back wheel. Ask someone to lift the back wheel while you slowly turn the pedals once. How many times does the wheel turn for each turn of the pedals?

**7** Get on your bike again and put it into a low gear. Repeat step 6. How many times did the wheel turn for one turn of the pedal this time?

Time to GEAR UP!

# A comfy ride

When the first bikes were made, their wheels were made of wood or iron with no tires. They were very uncomfortable to ride. Nowadays you have air-filled tires on your bike and maybe some suspension, either over the front wheel or at the front and the back. All these are ways of making your ride less bumpy. This easy experiment will show you how they work.

## You will need

A few tiny pieces of gravel

A chopping board

A rolling pin

A sheet of foam—either some thin foam rubber or the kind of foam sheeting you use under floors or sometimes find wrapped around new computers or electrical goods

Some sticky tape

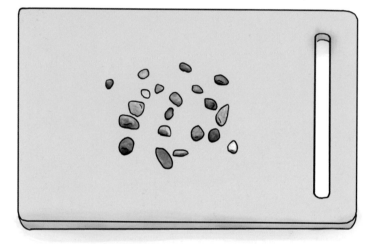

 **1** Sprinkle the pieces of gravel onto the chopping board.

 **2** Lightly roll the rolling pin over the gravel. Can you feel how bumpy it is?

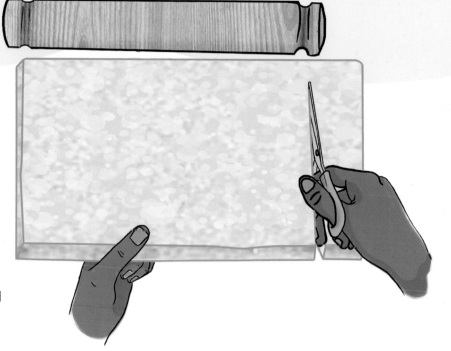

**3** Take the foam and cut a strip that is the same width as the rolling pin and long enough to wind round the rolling pin. If it is quite thick, winding it around once will be enough. If it is thin, cut it long enough to wind around at least three times.

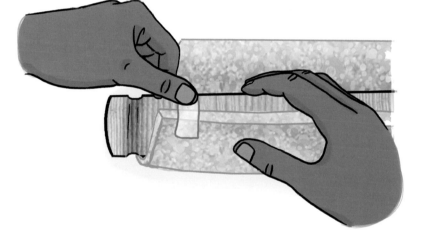

**4** Tape one end of the foam to the rolling pin.

**5** Wrap the rest of the foam tightly around the rolling pin. Secure the end with more sticky tape.

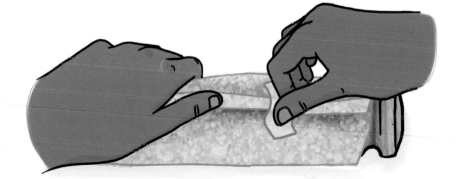

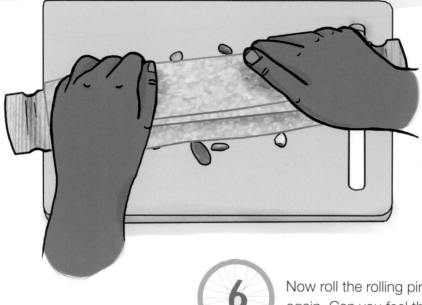

 **6** Now roll the rolling pin over the gravel again. Can you feel the gravel this time?

**7** The gravel has pushed up into the squashy foam and the rolling pin can keep rolling without bumping up and down. That's what happens with your tires and the suspension on your bike. The suspension is made of springs that can be pushed up just like the foam.

Who wants a B- B- BUMPY ride?

# Streamlining

Think of the Olympic cyclists. When they are cycling, they are always crouched low over dropped handlebars. They wear tight, shiny, stretchy suits and strange pointed helmets—why? For streamlining. To feel the effects of streamlining, try this simple experiment.

## You will need

A large sheet of card—the side of a large cardboard carton would do

A ruler

A pair of scissors or a blunt knife

 **1** Go outside so that you have space to run. Hold the card with both hands in front of you and run. Can you feel the air pressure pushing the card backward and bending it?

**2** Now fold the card down the middle. To get a good sharp fold, position the ruler down the middle and push firmly along the ruler with the point of the scissors or the knife, as if you are drawing a line. This is called scoring. It will dent the cardboard and make it easy to fold. Fold the card along the score line.

**3** Hold the card in front of you again, so that the point faces forward like the front of a ship. Run again. Did you find there was less pressure against the card this time? That's because the card was streamlined and cut easily through the air.

**4** Next time you are going fast down a hill, bend down low over your handlebars to streamline yourself and see how much faster you can go—but don't go so fast that you can't brake safely! (See page 28.)

Bend low and

ZOOM!

# Useful websites

For more information about bicycles, from training courses to events you could take part in, take a look at the websites below.

## US

### Safe Kids
Website promoting child safety, including safety on bikes.
www.safekids.org/safety-basics/safety-resources-by-risk-area/bicycling-and-skating

### League of American Bicyclists
Organization promoting cycling in the US, which also runs bike training courses for children.
www.bikeleague.org

### Trail Links
This links you to cycling trails in your area from the "Rails to Trails Conservancy," who are dedicated to creating a nationwide network of trails from former rail lines and connecting corridors.
www.traillink.com

### Adventure Cycling Association
They organize fully supported family fun tours for longer cycling adventures.
www.adventurecycling.org

### Department of Transportation
Email the "bicycling/pedestrian coordinator" at the Department of Transportation of your state to find a wealth of information, including maps of cycle routes and fun biking events in your locality.
www.dot.gov

## UK

### Bikeability
"Cycling proficiency for the 21st Century." This is the UK government cycle training scheme and is mostly delivered through schools.
www.dft.gov.uk/bikeability

### CTC
A national cycling charity that promotes cycling and has information about training courses and events suitable for children.
www.ctc.org.uk

### Sustrans
UK charity promoting sustainable transport, especially cycling. Click on the relevant links to find events and initiatives near you.
www.sustrans.org.uk

### National Cycle Network
A network of cycle routes in the UK created by Sustrans (see above), which can be downloaded as a smartphone app.
www.sustrans.org.uk/what-we-do/national-cycle-network

### British Cycling
The national governing body for cycling. Works with all levels of cycling and has details of clubs all over the country, including those that accept junior members.
www.britishcycling.org.uk

### Tales of the Road
A road safety website for kids, which includes cycling safety tips and a variety of online games.
talesoftheroad.direct.gov.uk

# Index

## Photography credits